CW00502187

1 MONTH OF
FREE
READING

at
www.ForgottenBooks.com

By purchasing this book you are eligible for one month membership to ForgottenBooks.com, giving you unlimited access to our entire collection of over 1,000,000 titles via our web site and mobile apps.

To claim your free month visit: www.forgottenbooks.com/free908672

ISBN 978-0-266-91221-7
PIBN 10908672

This book is a reproduction of an important historical work. Forgotten Books uses
state-of-the-art technology to digitally reconstruct the work, preserving the original format
whilst repairing imperfections present in the aged copy. In rare cases, an imperfection in
the original, such as a blemish or missing page, may be replicated in our edition. We do,
however, repair the vast majority of imperfections successfully; any imperfections that
remain are intentionally left to preserve the state of such historical works.

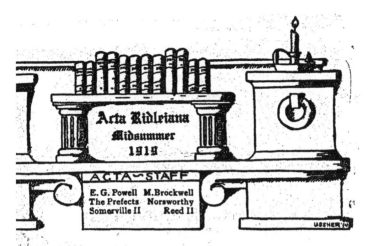

Acta Ridleiana
Midsummer
1919

A.CTA~STAFF
E. G. Powell   M. Brockwell
The Prefects   Norsworthy
Somerville II   Reed II

EDITORIAL

⁋R School Year has flown quickly by, and with it Rid-
ollege completes the thirtieth year of its history, the
:rous year of all, in which the School has for the first
⁊o hundred names on its roll. Numbers alone would
'ant any great satisfaction, but when we realize that
has been steady, and our reputation such as to invite
ıce of an ever-increasing number of friends, we have
of which we may all feel justly proud.

ar we are sending out a large number of our oldest
ɾe feel confident that the impression they will make
'ther enhance the good name we have earned in the

r years, since 1914, our boys left School to go into the
ıt without exception, and the record these have made
ɾes and their school has added not a little to the lustre
ı name.

e sixty who sacrificed their life in the cause for which
ıting, it may, in all truth be said they were of our best,
ames and deeds will live forever as an example for
ɛians.

ɪ thankful, in saying au revoir to those leaving this
ɾe do not face the same possibility of it being a real
ıd we wish them all a prosperous future in this coun-
in which they and their generation must do so much
ɪ full harvest, which those have made possible, who
:rom us beyond recall.

THE TERM

ıst term, as usual, has kept us fully employed, and
⁊een scarcely time to crowd in the many activities.

The work of the School has, on the whole, been well done from the lower forms to the sixth, and much of the time lost on account of "flu" last fall has been made up.

The various competitions, such as that for the Leonard Essay Prize, the Speaking Prize, and the Reading Prize brought out in each case, a large number of competitors, whose efforts were well up to the high standards of other years.

The outside activities were many and varied. Cadet Corps drill took up much time in the early part of the term, and was so well attended to by all that our Annual Inspection was a great success. Cricket claimed the attention of nearly every one, but a very few tennis enthusiasts, and it was no uncommon thing to have six games going on at once in addition to the first-net practice.

The Tennis Tournament (doubles) was run off between times, and thirty-six of the upper formers (fifth and sixth) entered.

The Annual Games, as usual, provided several afternoons' sport, and on the last day the finals provided an interesting entertainment to many friends of the School from town and out-of-town.

The Shooting and Swimming Contests were entered by large numbers, and the various winners had no easy path to travel in securing the coveted honour of first place.

We regret to announce the departure from our Staff of Rev. W. L. Archer, who has been with us since last December. Our good wishes follow him to his new work in Hamilton, whither he has been called by the Bishop of Niagara to take charge of St. James' Church.

Mr. Rowan and Mr. Tait will continue their work at the University next year, and both of these gentlemen will be missed by boys and staff.

We are sorry that Mrs. H. J. Flynn, who has been School-nurse since Mr. Flynn's death, is leaving Ridley to resume private nursing in Hamilton. Our best wishes go with her.

It is expected that Mr. Bright, who left us to go to the war, will be a member of the Staff when School re-opens in September, and we shall welcome him into our midst again.

Sport—Why do they paint the inside of chicken coops?
Rube—I dunno.
Sport—To keep the hens from picking the grain out of the wood.

SCHOOL BOY SOCIALISM

A T least we have one thing to be thankful for these days—the Bolshie bacteria has not yet pervaded our school system.

Did it ever occur to you how it would feel, if one morning you read in your breakfast Globe, some such item as this: "Serious outbreak of Revolutionary Flags at Ridley College—Red Flag Hoisted in the Head Master's. Study—Ring Leaders Refuse to Shave, and Come Down to Breakfast Without Collars."

It is not until we picture such scenes as these, that we realize the shaky foundation upon which our school system stands. Masters, in fits of intellectual fury, award punishments right and left; prefects think they are the only people entitled to shave with straight razors; gymnasium instructors won't allow people to swim in the tank until the water is thoroughly dirty, and a fellow can't requisition more than one Christy hat per term. Are these conditions such as befit the upbringing of future independent Canadian citizens? Are we not, at times, too autocratic with our pupils or juniors—are there not many musty and out-of-date customs and methods of procedure with which he could easily dispense?

Take for instance the Requisition. I can picture the many brilliant, sun-shiny afternoons upon which I have sat in my despicable form-room and foregone that tutti-frutti sundae at the Lorraine, that I might get my little slip signed by which I hoped to secure a new undershirt. In these times of big business, filing systems and chocolate eggnogs, we need a better, speedier and more flexible system. Give me the days when you can tear into Louis Bissonnette's and say, "Slip us some natty neckwear and charge it up to the old man!"

Then our pocket-money. Look at it. I ask you, what is thirty-five cents in these days of billion-dollar indemnities? How can we treat the Collegiate "Not Outs" from King street at the Blue Bird? From where are we to get our scented Palmolive and the weekly Cosmo from the Bookshop? How can a chap keep up appearances such as are worthy of a Fourth-Former on such a pittance?

Then our meals. Ah, yes! Our meals. Time, expense and worry could easily be saved by the adoption of an ultra-modern method by which eating is reduced to such a science that all you have to do is to move your jaws up and down. Let us picture a huge tiled dining-room, steaming counters behind which the beaming face of a real chef would greet us with a curt: "What's yours?" to which the boys would reply with such refined and established curtesies as :"Two baled hay," "Fish Eggs and Glue," "Rare beef soaked in paint," and other cognomens by which our Ridley menu has since time immemorial been recognized.

If we can be spared another instance, let us look at improvement from the time-table standpoint. Although many will disagree with me when I say it, we do not rise too early. We are not awakened too early—but too rudely. The jarring notes of an electric bell certainly never could be musical at seven a.m. (much worse under the new time). The modern youth would respond much more readily were he not so provoked. In winter, at 6.30, an automatic device should quietly close the window at the same time that the heat comes through the pipes. When the radiators had reached a satisfactory temperature, the steam by escaping through a valve would sound a pleasant whistle, which would keep up, peanut-like, until turned off. Breakfast on the cafeteria system, with a pile of trays, which would give out about 7.50, in order that those who came later would be out of luck. Chapel in the good old style, except that instead of a prefect calling the roll, everybody would punch the time-clock as he entered.

Instead of all the comparatively useless subjects to which we are now subjected, the time-table would read like this:

9 a.m.-10.15—The Pelman System.

10.15-11.30—Practical Demonstration and Instructions in the use of a McLaughlin Car.

11.30-12.30—Life Studies of Prominent Movie Actors.

2.30-3.15—Popular music under the Marks-Winn System. Piano, ukulele and guitar.

3.15-3.45—Instructive Lectures by Famous People, Such as Wm. S. Hart, Al. Tolson and Newsy Lalonde.

The numerous other instances which we could set out our space is too limited to hold. But suffice it to say that the undercurrent of reform is not entirely hidden by the smooth running surface water and it behooves those in authority to devote statesman-like consideration to direct our progress in equitable channels such as have been set out. And to soothe the fears of any who feel an immediate outbreak upon us, it will be wise to add that as far as we can make out from the conversation of the Flat, Happy Eight and Forty-Below, there is nothing organized yet, and, anyway, the holidays are here.

A TRUE WAR STORY

THE wily and alert Editor of this magazine, taking advantage of my visit to the School, seized me by the collar in the Masters' study, and demanded of me a written account of my doings in Germany, to be ready for the midsummer number. Wriggling away and settling my tie again, I promised to do the best I could in such short order, but, like the burglar upon whom the grandfather's clock had just fallen, I find that time presses. Were I to write a long and detailed account of my imprisonment in Germany, I should still be working on it when midsummer came, so I must abbreviate and limit myself to one experience—an experience that may not appear funny to the reader, but which tickles my sense of humour delightfully and has caused many a laugh among my fellow prisoners.

There were six prisoners journeying in a fourth-class carriage from the distribution camp in Courtrai, Belgium, to the permanent camp at Rastatt, Germany. One of them, an American flying man, announced his intention of taking the first opportunity that presented itself, to escape. He said this quite openly, knowing that the two guards who sat in the same carriage with us did not understand a word of English.

About eleven o'clock that night the train was creeping (Belgian trains always creep) along the border line of Holland, not more than eight or nine miles from the frontier. Inside the carriage, everyone sat huddled up in a state of coma, tired out by the eternal and infernal jogging of the slow train, and stiff and sore from sitting on the hard seats for twelve hours without a break. Even the guards who should have been alert and watchful, dozed in their places next to the window.

Suddenly I awoke from a slight snooze and sat upright. Perfect quietness reigned in the carriage. I put out my left arm and tried to find a soft spot in the anatomy of the person who sat next to me, in order to rest my head upon it. The corner was empty. The dawn was just beginning to brighten outstanding features in the landscape, and by its light I could now see that instead of eight people, only seven now occupied the carriage—five prisoners and two guards. I awaited developments.

One of the guards started upright and rubbed his eyes. He also looked round the carriage sleepily. He took another look and I saw him galvanize to attention. Then he awoke his fellow sentry and they both searched high and low, with the aid of a flashlight. Outside in the corridor they hunted, but all to no purpose. The American had made his get-away in fine style!

By this time we were all wide awake and chuckling to ourselves. Roberts (the American) had certainly done it pretty
smoothly, not to wake one of us during the escape. We saw now
that he had crept out while the Huns slumbered and had climbed
out of a small window in the corridor.

One of the guards now fetched the Sergeant-Major in charge
of the party, who had been sitting in another carriage. He came
dashing in, his automatic in hand, and began yelling at us at the
top of his voice. Thanks to my four years of German at Ridley,
I gathered that he wanted to know how our friend had escaped.
The man became more and more excited and waved his beastly
revolver round the compartment savagely. I sat next to the door
and my spine wriggled every time the muzzle pointed my way.
The pistol had a hair-trigger.

Plucking up courage I yelled "Wir schliefen! Wir schliefen"
(we were sleeping), meaning to tell him that we knew nothing
about it, being asleep at the time of the escape. The more I said
it, the louder the man raved, and my four companions took up the
cry after me, so that the carriage rang with "Wir schliefens"
and the yells of the Germans.

Finally peace was restored and the sergeant-major left the
compartment and a minute later the train was stopped and a
search took place, but no sign of Roberts was found, so we again
started off and about seven o'clock drew into a small town where
we were hustled off the train and lined up on the platform. Then
the sergeant-major, to show us he meant business, made the
guards load their rifles in our faces, as much as to say, "One
move and you'll be shot, me lad." Then he marched us to another
platform and I noticed that he kept his hand on the butt of his
revolver and eyed us ferociously. I verily believe, had one of us
slipped on a banana peeling, he would have riddled that man. He
meant business.

To cut a long tale short, we learned here that Roberts had
been captured and we were to wait till the next train brought him
to the station, when we would all journey on again together.
The news put a kink in our elation, for we had been sure that the
Yank had got clear away.

It turned out that he had jumped off the train just as it
entered a tunnel, and after picking himself up again, he had
plunged on after it, meaning to follow it out of the tunnel and
then to run cross country. He might have known that all tun-
nels were carefully guarded by the Huns. As it was, he ran into
the arms of a sentry, who promptly shoved his rifle in his face
and marched him off to his commanding officer.

The rest of our journey was uneventful, and Roberts was forbidden to speak to us at all. He was also watched closely all the way. When we arrived at Rastatt he was put in solitary confinement as punishment and was kept there for several days.

—E. H. B.

Speaking Contest

Not so many as usual entered the speaking contest this year, but the subjects were exceedingly interesting and very instructive. Several visitors came over from the city for the evening. Each competitor spoke on a chosen subject first and later spoke extemporaneously on a subject given by Dr. Miller. Among the topics and speakers: "George Washington" (Peixotto); "Birds," (Perkins); "Remedies for Labor," (Stringer ma.); "Paying Off the War Debt," (Gilchrist); "Russian Revolutions," (Tebbs); "The Solar System," (Greentree); "Trade and Industry," (Soanes); "The Peace Terms," (Norsworthy).

The Judges decided that Norsworthy was the winner of the first prize, Dr. Merritt's Gold Locket, while Stringer ma. came second, winning the gold cuff links donated by Mr. Kingstone. Owing to the very excellent impression created by Greentree (III.A.), who spoke on "The Solar System," a special third prize was awarded to him.

SPORTS DAY

WITH ideal weather, and many more visitors than usual, the annual games were held on the athletic field on Friday, May 30th, with a very large number taking part in each event. On this account many heats were necessary, and the committee in charge is to be congratulated on running off the long list with no confusion or delay.

This year the Senior Championship was won by W. A. Woodruff, with a total of 38 points, Barr being second with 16. D. L. McWhinney won the Intermediate with 31, and Shurly the Junior with 23. The Lower School Championship was won by Fairbank.

Following the events, Mrs. W. Hamilton Merritt presented the prizes, after which refreshments were served on the grounds.

Among the visitors from out-of-town were: Mr. and Mrs. W. J. McWhniney and Miss McWhinney, Mr. and Mrs. Alfred Rogers, Mrs. W. A. H. Kerr, Col. G. G. Mitchell, Mrs. Warren, Mr. W. C. Brent, Miss Scott, Mrs. Osler, Mrs. H. Willan, Col. and Mrs. W. H. Merritt (Toronto), Mrs. S. J. Macey (Avon, N. Y.), Mr. and Mrs. W. M. Bright (Niagara Falls), Mr. Grant (Ottawa), Mr. and

Mrs. H. E. Gates, Mrs. C. R. Somerville (London), Mr. and Mrs. Sims (Kitchener), Mr. and Mrs. Snyder (Waterloo), Mr. and Mrs. E. M. Weaver, Mr. G. A. Forbes (Hespeler), Mrs. R. R. Wallace, Mrs. Geo. Hope, Mr. and Mrs. J. A. and Miss Henderson, Mrs. Stringer (Hamilton), Mr. A. R. Goldie, Mr. J. Goldie, Mr. L. McCulloch, Mr. J. Todd (Galt), Miss Marlatt, and Mr. and Mrs. Law, (Oakville).

The full results were as follows:

Running Broad Jump	* Rogers	Woodruff	Eager	
	‡ McWhinney	Stewart	Baker	
	† Shurly	Douglas	Peixotto	
Running High Jump	* Rogers	Gilchrist	Barr	
	‡ Bright mi	McWhinnney	Douglas	
	† Douglas	Bright mi	Shurly	
Running Half Mile	* Woodruff	Baird	Stringer ma	
	‡ McWhinney	Baker	Gordon I	
	† Shurly	Thompson	Bright mi	
Running One Mile	* Woodruff	Baird	Shurly	
Running Quarter Mile	* Gilchrist	Woodruff	Barr	
	‡ McWhinney	Baker	Stewart	
	† Shurly	Thompson	Bright mi	
Running 100 Yards	* Woodruff	Barr	Soanes	
	‡ McWhinney	Stewart	Baker	
	† Thompson	Shurly	Bright mi	
Running 220 Yards	* Woodruff	Barr	Orme	
	‡ McWhinney	Baker	Stringer mi	
	† Thompson	Shurly	Bright mi	
Hurdle Race	* Rogers	Andrews	Woodruff	
	‡ Stewart	McWhinney	Baker	
	† Douglas	Thompson		
Three-legged Race	* Stanworth and Andrews			
	‡ Magness and Smith (under 15)			
Relay Race	Prefects—Barr, Moore Stringer ma, Soanes			
	VI—Burton, Norsworthy, Bertram, Woodruff			
Consolation, 100 Yards	* Johnston I			
	‡ Campbell			
Running 100 Yards (under 12)..	Case	Davies	Robins	
Running 100 Yards (under 11)..	Kinnear	Hislop mi	Stringer mi	
Running 100 Yards (under 13)..	DeWitt	Neeve	Newman	
Running 100 Yards (under 14)..	Fairbank	Hislop ma	Barnett	
Running 220 Yards	Fairbank	Hislop ma	Barnett	
Three-legged Race	Mather and Milledge; Grobba and Cronyn			

Events marked * count for Senior Championship, ‡ Intermediate Champ., † Junior Champ.

The Rink

The contractors have been busy during the term with the finishing touches to the rink, and now, with stucco walls and fresh paint, it presents a most pleasing appearance.

The interior has also been completed and the new armoury for the Cadet Corps fills a long-felt want.

The dirt floor will be rolled and may be used for indoor tennis if necessity arise for more courts than we have at present.

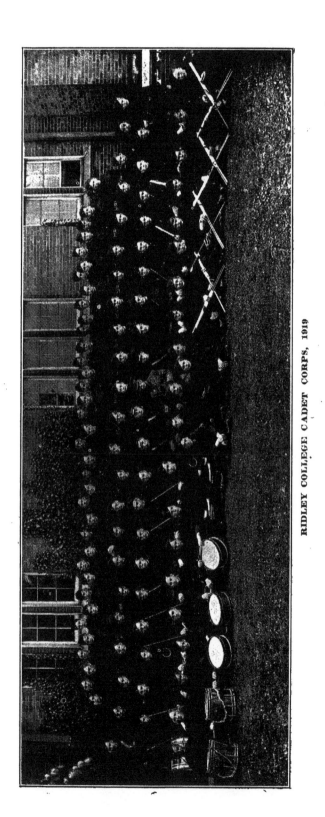

RIDLEY COLLEGE CADET CORPS, 1919

THE CRICKET SEASON

THE Cricket Season has been most successful in every way, and practically the whole School has been engaged every afternoon in learning the fine points of the game.

Every form in the Upper School has been represented in inter-form matches, and much good material for future teams has been developed.

Those on the first net practiced steadily, and we feel that our first three elevens have been quite up to the average of our best years.

Few matches were lost with outside elevens, and we can look forward to the next few years with the comfortable feeling that there is plenty of excellent material available for our first elevens.

To bring back the School Championship, was in itself an achievement worth while, and as we expect a number of our old colours back, we have hopes that we may be strong enough to keep our honours next year.

ALBIONS vs. RIDLEY

The season opened on May 17th, when the Albion Club of Toronto paid us a visit. Keen enthusiasts they were, as the day was decidedly not a promising one, and our ground was very wet from continuous rain.

After lunch a start was made, and the visitors, who had come to us without practice, were all out for 56.

Ridley did much better and on a drying wicket scored 105 before the last wicket fell. Barr batted well for his 29, while Johnson, MacMahon and Harrison all reached double figures.

ALBION		RIDLEY	
Blackman, c Williams, b Somerville	6	MacMahon, l b w Roberts	15
Wakefield, c Biggar, b Saunders	13	Somerville, b Yaxley	2
Rogers, run out	3	Harrison, l b w Hall	12
Glass, run out	9	Woodruff, c and b Yaxley	3
Yaxley, b Saunders	2	Barr, b Smith	29
Adams, b Biggar I.	6	Williams, l b w Wakefield	4
Hall, b Woodruff	10	Saunders, b Hall	1
Walmsley, b Woodruff	2	O'Brian, c Walmsley, b Wakefield	3
Smith, b Woodruff	0	Johnston I., not out	19
Belgrave, run out	4	Stringer, b Adams	8
Roberts, not out	0	Biggar I., c Wakefield, b Roberts	2
Extras	1	Extras	7
Total	56	Total	105

OLD COUNTRY CLUB vs. RIDLEY

Our annual match with an eleven chosen by Mr. Dean for May 24th, brought the strong Old Country team of Toronto to visit us this year.

Again the wicket was soft and in the bowlers' favour, so that scores were low.

Ridley went in first, but could do little with the bowling of Greene and McKinnon, and the side was out for 44.

Old Country followed, but were never able to master our bowling and were quickly retired for 47.

Ridley in a second attempt did much better, and put on 73 for 6, of which Barr made 40 in good style.

Old Country replied with 36 for 4, playing out time, and winning on the first innings by three runs.

OLD COUNTRY CLUB		OLD COUNTRY CLUB, 2nd Innings	
Heath, run out	4	Heath, c and b Somerville	4
Lowen, l b w Woodruff	6	McKinnon, b Saunders	0
Greene, b Somerville I.	5	Greene, not out	11
Wakefield, c Johnston, b Woodruff	6	Wakefield, b Somerville	19
Downer, b Somerville	12	Lowen, c Stringer, b Woodruff..	1
Bowbanks, c Johnston, b Somerville	4	Bowbanks, not out	1
Barford, c Harrison, b O'Brian.	5	Barford	
McKinnon, s Somerville	5	Downer	
Cameron, l b w Somerville....	0	Camerson } Did not bat.	
Henderson, c Harrison, b Woodruff	0	Henderson	
S. Mix, not out	0		
Total	47	Total	36

RIDLEY		RIDLEY, 2nd Innings	
MacMahon, b McKinnon	4	Williams, c Wakefield, b Lowen	0
Somerville, b Greene	3	O'Brian, c McKinnon, b Wakefield	7
Harrison, b McKinnon	3	Harrison, c McKinnon, b Wakefield	3
Woodruff, b Greene	3	Saunders, c Henderson, b Wakefield	3
Barr, c and b Greene	5	Barr, b McKinnon	40
Williams, c McKinnon	4	Somerville, not out	12
O'Brian, c McKinnon	7	Woodruff, b McKinnon	1
Saunders, c McKinnon	5	Johnston, c McKinnon	0
Johnston, c Greene	1	MacMahon	
Soanes, b McKinnon	3	Soanes } Did not bat.	
Stringer, not out	0	Stringer	
Extras	4	Extras	3
Total	44	Total	73

YORKSHIRE vs. RIDLEY

The visit of the Yorkshire Society Cricket Club on Saturday, May 31st, resulted in our eleven obtaining some very valuable experience and incidentally a bad beating.

The bowling of Murray and Marsden, on a bowlers' wicket, proved too much for our players, and Baird (21) was the only one to reach double figures, the side being dismissed for 48 runs.

Yorkshire did much better and gathered together an even 100 runs, of which Marsden contributed 31, and Greenwood 29.

RIDLEY, 1st Innings		RIDLEY, 2nd Innings	
MacMahon, b Murray	4	Somerville I., not out	15
O'Brian, run out	0	Barr, c Greenwood, b Pickard	6
Somerville I., b Marsden	1	Harrison ma., b Joy	1
Harrison ma., b Marsden	8	Woodruff, not out	17
Barr, c Greenwood, b Murray	4	Baird	
Woodruff, b Marsden	0	Johnston I.	
Williams, s Marsden	0	MacMahon	
Baird, c Childs, b Murray	21	Williams	Did not bat.
Johnston I., b Murray	1	O'Brian	
Saunders I., not out	2	Saunders I.	
Soanes, b Murray	5	Soanes	
Extras	2	Extras	3
Total	48	Total	42

YORKSHIRE CLUB

Kerslake, b Woodruff	12	T. Preistley, b Somerville	0
Joy, c O'Brian, b Woodruff	2	Brodziak, c Woodruff, b Somerville	0
Greenwood, c Barr, b Saunders	29	Pickard, b Saunders	10
J. Priestley, c Harrison, b O'Brian	11	Nutter, b MacMahon	3
Marsden, not out	31	Extras	2
Murray, c MacMahon, b Saunders	0		
Child's, b Somerville	0	Total	100

OLD BOYS vs. RIDLEY

The Old Boys visited the School on Saturday, June 7th, and put a very strong eleven in the field, composed of old colours, almost without exception.

R. M. Harcourt and Hugh McCulloch went in first, and for a time it looked as if the School bowling was not good enough, the runs came so fast. McCulloh mi., A. L. and W. S. Greening, kept up the good work, as did Eric Lefroy and Mill Jarvis. The latter is not quite so quick as in former years, and was run out after getting nicely started. Geof. Marani, Geo. Marks, C. Hyde, Hollis Blake, Ed. Riselay, all added to the score, and the School was lucky in retiring the old fellows for 135.

Hugh McCulloch's 52 was a fine exhibition, and indicates that artillery work in no way dims the eye.

The present boys faced the bowling of Greening and Lefroy, who were very effective until Barr and MacMahon made a fine stand, the former coming within one of equalling McCulloch's efforts. With 39 to his credit, MacMahon was out on what looked like a bump ball. Glass put on a very useful 9, and with the extras the side just equalled the score of their older adversaries, an exciting end to a very interesting game.

OLD BOYS		RIDLEY	
Harcourt, c Williams, b Somerville	14	MacMahon, c McCulloch, b Greening	39
McCulloch, b O'Brian	?	Somerville, c Harcourt, b Lefroy	6
H. McCulloch, b O'Brian	52	Harrison, b Greening	0
A. L. McCulloch, c Williams, b MacMahon	15	Barr, c McCulloch, b Lefroy	51
Greening, c Baird, b Harrison	5	Baird, b Lefroy	4
Lefroy, b MacMahon	11	Williams, run out	2
Marani, b Somerville	6	O'Brian, b Lefroy	5
Jarvis, run out	9	Johnston, c Lefroy, b Greening	1
Marks, s Barr, b MacMahon	1	Glass, not out	9
Hyde, c MacMahon, b O'Brian	7	Moore, b Lefroy	0
Blake, c Glass, b Harrison	10	Soanes, c Riseley, b Lefroy	0
Riseley, not out	4	Extras	18
Extras	5		
Total	135	Total	135

ST. GEORGE'S vs. RIDLEY

St. George's Cricket Club, Hamilton, sent an eleven to the School on Wednesday, June 11th, and found our eleven in excellent condition.

The visitors batted first and put on about 60 runs for the two wickets, which seemed like a fine start. The next two men added only 15 more and then came the collapse, the last six wickets adding only about 10 more, so that the side was out for 85.

McMahon and Somerville commenced for Ridley, and both did good work, the former's 43 being a good exhibition of careful cricket.

Barr made 48, not out, Glass 23 retired, Williams 23, and O'Brian 7, not out, and the side declared for 180, and sent the visitors in for a second inning, which netted them 69 runs, Nutt being high again with 18.

Somerville and O'Brian both bowled well for Ridley, the former taking 10 wickets in the two innings.

ST. GEORGE'S, 1st Innings		ST. GEORGE'S, 2nd Innings	
Wise, c Barr, b O'Brian	8	Wise, s Barr, b Somerville	1
Nutt, run out	31	Budd, b Somerville	1
Robinson, c Johnston, b O'Brian	17	Nutt, b Somerville	18
Stewart, c Baird, b Somerville	4	Richmond, b Somerville	11
Budd, run out	11	Stewart, c Moore, b Baird	0
Richmond, c Williams, b O'Brian	0	Davis, s Barr, b Somerville	15
Davis, c O'Brian, b Somerville	1	Collinson, b Somerville	0
Collinson, b Somerville	0	Robinson, c O'Brian, b Somerville	10
Hulford, not out	7	Hulford, run out	8
Greening mi., b O'Brian	0	Greening mi., c O'Brian, b Baird	0
Westgate, run out	0	Westgate, not out	0
Extras	6	Extras	5
Total	85	Total	69

RIDLEY

MacMahon, retired, not out....	43	Stringer		
Somerville, b Stewart	15	Norsworthy		
Barr, not out	48	Moore	Did not bat	
Baird, c Davis, b Budd	5	Johnston		
Glass, retired, not out.........	23	Extras		16
Williams, b Wise	23			
O'Brian, not out	7	Total		180

ST. ANDREW'S vs. RIDLEY

The first School match was played in Toronto on the University Campus against S. A. C. on June 14th, and resulted in an easy win for Ridley.

St. Andrew's went in first, with Hewitt (Capt.) and Cameron opening, and the pair played steady cricket until Somerville caught the latter off Woodruff. Hewitt continued to make runs until he was l b w at 21, and then wickets fell rapidly until the last, where a short stand by Robertson carried the score to 46.

Early in the innings Barr had to retire owing to a nasty blow on the eye, and his inability to go on might have been serious had the teams been more evenly matched. As it turned out, we were quite strong enough to win, and the emergency proved the worth of Glass as a substitute wicket keeper.

Somerville and MacMahon opened for Ridley and were playing well when MacMahon was caught at point. O'Brian and Woodruff followed, but did not do much, and it was only when Somerville was joined by Williams that the real stand of the match took place. Somerville (47) was finally caught in the long field, while Williams, after a good exhibition, tried to pull a straight one and was bowled.

Glass and Baird were going nicely, when a heavy rain storm stopped the game, with Ridley in the lead by 105 for 5 to 46.

The thanks of the team is extended to Dr. and Mrs. MacDonald, who did so much to make the visit of Ridley to St. Andrew's a pleasant remembrance.

ST. ANDREW'S

Hewitt, l b w Woodruff	21
Cameron, c Somerville, b Woodruff	4
Clift, b Woodruff	0
Auld, c Johnston, b Woodruff..	1
Lyon, l b w Saunders	4
Rendell, b O'Brian	1
King, b Woodruff	5
Findlay, c Williams, b Saunders	0
Clark, not out	4
Robertson, b Somerville	7
Stirrett, l b w O'Brian	0
Extras	4
Total	46

RIDLEY

Somerville I., c Hewitt, b Auld.	47	
MacMahon, c Cameron, b Auld.	7	
O'Brian, c and b Clark.........	5	
Barr (hurt)		
Woodruff, b Clift	3	
Williams, b Robertson	25	
Glass, not out	5	
Baird, not out	6	
Saunders I.		
Soanes	Did not bat.	
Johnston I.		
Stringer		
Did not bat		
Extras	7	
Total 105		

HAVERFORD vs. RIDLEY

Haverford College C. C. visited Ridley for an all-day match on Monday, June 16th, and were defeated in an interesting game by 181 to 107.

The visitors batted first, and began well, but with the fall of their first two batsmen for 18, a rot set in, and owing to excellent bowling by Somerville, we had 8 wickets down for 59. The last two men put on 48 runs by free hitting and good running, and the final score was 107.

Ridley opened badly and lost two wickets for 10 runs, but Mr. Harper by careful play stopped the procession, and with Williams and Glass as successive partners carried the score to 95. O'Brian, Saunders and Johnson all did good work, and the side was finally dismissed for the respectable total of 181 runs. Haverford arrived at Ridley on Sunday evening, and the visitors were entertained at the School until Tuesday morning, when they left for Toronto. We all enjoyed their visit, and hope to be able to accept their cordial invitation to play a return match at Haverford in the near future.

HAVERFORD COLLEGE		RIDLEY	
Porter, b O'Brian	18	MacMahon, b Thorpe	7
Crosman, b Woodruff	10	Somerville, c Toogood, b Thorpe	1
Rogers, b Somerville	3	Harper, c and b Thorpe	43
Thornton, hit wicket	5	Barr, b Crossman	14
Toogood, b Somerville	5	Woodruff, c and b Crossman	0
Kearney, b Woodruff	11	Williams, b Crossman	12
Carey, b Woodruff	6	Glass, c Nicholson, b Crossman	34
Thorpe, c O'Brian, b Somerville	1	Baird, c Porter, b Thorpe	0
Abell, b O'Brian	17	O'Brian, b Toogood	17
Nicholson, b Somerville	24	Saunders I., b Carey	20
Ewan, not out	7	Johnson, not out	15
		Extras	15
Total	67	Total	181

U. C. S. vs. RIDLEY

The annual match with U. C. C. was played this year on our own ground, and resulted in a good win for Ridley after an interesting game.

Batting first, U. C. C. played careful cricket, Beatty 54, Richards 12, Cross 15, being those to reach doubles, of a total of 108.

MacMahon and Somerville opened for Ridley, and put on 48 for the first wicket. Somerville's clean hit for six was a beautiful pull to leg of a full pitch. Barr batted splendidly and retired at 55. Glass, MacMahon and O'Brian also did well, and the game was won with 5 wickets down. Ridley played out time, and in the end made 170 for 9 wickets.

For Ridley Somerville took 5 wickets for 49, while Woodruff got 4 for 33.

RIDLEY		U. C. C.	
MacMahon, run out	21	Short, b Somerville	2
Somerville, c and b Greey	34	Richards, b Woodruff	12
Harrison, b Cross	6	Dean, b Woodruff	0
Barr, retired	55	Swabey, b Somerville	6
Woodruff, b Phillips	3	Beatty, b Somerville	54
Williams, b Phillips	2	Cross, b O'Brian	15
O'Brian, b Zybach	10	Greey, b Woodruff	1
Glass, l b w Beatty	22	Winslow, b Woodruff	8
Saunders, b Zybach	5	Zybach, b Somerville	2
Baird, not out	8	White, b Somerville	3
Johnston I., did not bat		Phillips, not out	1
Extras	4	Extras	4
Total	170	Total	108

T. C. S. vs. RIDLEY

The final game of the season was played against T. C. S. on U. C. C. grounds, and resulted in a close and exciting match, Ridley winning, and thereby bringing back the championship once more.

Batting first, T. C. S. with the exception of Cumberland 36, could do little with our bowling, and were all out before lunch for 65 runs.

Ridley started well, and with Somerville and MacMahon at the wickets, carried the score to 40 before the first wicket fell. Somerville again made a fine hit for 6. The second wicket fell for 47, and then a number of l b w decisions changed the complexion entirely, and with 8 down for 57, it was any one's game.

Saunders saved the day by good hard batting, and his confident play carried the score beyond 65. Woodruff was run out, and the last wicket fell for 77, of which Somerville 35, MacMahon 13, Saunders 15, were those to reach double figures.

T. C. S.		RIDLEY	
Rees, b Woodruff	0	MacMahon, l b w Kaulbach	13
Petry, b Somerville	4	Somerville, c Ross, b Jones	35
Cumberland, c MacMahon, b Saunders	36	O'Brian, b Cumberland	5
Nickle, b Woodruff	2	Barr, c Smith, b Cumberland	0
Grout, c O'Brian, b Woodruff	0	Glass, l b w Nickle	0
Jones, c Woodruff, b Somerville	2	Harrison ma., l b w Cumberland	1
Coyley, b O'Brian	3	Williams, l b w Brown	1
Brown, c Barr, b O'Brian	0	Baird, b Brown	3
Brown, c Barr, b O'Brian	0	Saunders, b Jones	15
Kaulbach, not out	7	Woodruff, run out	2
Smith, l b w O'Brian	7	Johnston, not out	2
Greaves, c O'Brian, b Saunders	1		
Extras	3		
Total	65	Total	77

THE ELEVEN.

The present season ended most successfully, and the eleven well deserved the honours won—the Championship.

When cricket commenced, a long spell of wet weather made practice anything but pleasant, but for the last month weather conditions were ideal, and good progress was made under MacMahon (Captain). There was keen competition for the five places to be filled, and some of the new colours have already shown their value.

In batting the eleven was strong, while in fielding and bowling quite up to the average. Between wickets fewer mistakes were made than usual, and in all the finer points of the game, the eleven showed good knowledge.

The visit of Haverford College was an innovation, and we hope that in future tours of the same eleven, we may have the pleasure of entertaining them. Possibly we may have an opportunity of playing a return game, when Matriculation dates once more permit of our annual tour.

MacMahon (Capt.)—Second year on the eleven. Has improved wonderfully in all departments of the game, and while not a forcing bat, was nearly always a sure run getter. Captained his team well, and had their full confidence.

Barr—Third year on the eleven. Has developed into a fine bat and was excellent behind the wickets. His average for the season of 31.5 won him first place in the batting averages, while two scores of over 50, and one of 48, not out, indicate clearly his soundness.

Woodruff—Third year on the eleven. An excellent bowler, and at times a forcing bat, but not quite up to expectations. His absence during the R. M. C. examinations probably had much to do with his failure to make runs, and next year he should do much better.

Somerville—Third year on the eleven. Has improved in all departments and is already a fine cricketer. His bowling was excellent, and won for him the bowling average, while in batting he was second to Barr, with an average of 19.

Harrison—Second year on the eleven. A change bowler, and a fair bat of the forcing order. His season was interrupted by examinations, which had much to do with his failure to make good scores.

Williams—Second year on the eleven. A fine, sharp fielder at point, and should with care develop into a good bat. Has a cramped style, which interferes with his hitting, and which it is hoped may be improved next year.

UPPER SCHOOL SNAPS

—First year on the eleven. He has developed into
er, and a very fair bat; also fields well.
rs—First year on the eleven. A very promising player.
and with more experience should be invaluable. Is a
; bat, and his stand in the T. C. S. game practically
itch.
First year on the eleven. A good, sound left hand
ery good wicket keeper. He has proved himself well
lace.
1—First year on the eleven. A very promising player,
s place for his fine fielding, and has improved with
l.
First year on the eleven. A very promising left hand
;ood, steady bowler. He should be of great value next

FIRST ELEVEN RECORD.

'—Albions at Ridley........................Won
l—Old Country at Ridley..................Lost
l—Yorkshire at Ridley....................Lost
'—Old Boys at Ridley......................Tie
.—St. George's at Ridley..................Won
l—S. A. C. at Toronto.....................Won
l—Haverford College at Ridley............Won
l—U. C. C. at Ridley ....Won
l—T. C. S. at Toronto.....................Won
.ampions, '13, '14, '15, '16, '17, '19-

BATTING AVERAGES

	A.B.	N.O.	R.	H.S.	Aver.
....	10	2	252	55*	31.5
....	6	3	93	34	31
)n	9	1	153	43*	19.1
le	11	2	171	47	10
....	7	3	42	19*	10.5
....	7	2	47	21	9.4
l	7	1	51	20	7.3
....	10	0	73	25	7.3
....	10	1	66	17	7.3
....	8	0	38	12	4.7
t	9	1	32	17*	4

BOWLING AVERAGES

	W.	R.	Aver.
ierville	36	242	6.7
)druff	24	180	7.5
nders	10	95	9.5
rian	17	191	11.2
Mahon	4	52	13
rd	2	30	15

Second Team

On May 24th the IInd's met a picked junior team from the Albion, Old Country and Yorkshire Clubs. In the first inning they were all out for 38 runs, while Ridley made 102. The Toronto boys were all out for 26 in the second innings, and the IInd's had 8 for 38 when stumps were drawn.

TORONTO, 1st Innings.	
Robinson, b Biggar I.	12
Baxter, l b w Biggar II.	8
Stockdale, b Biggar I.	3
Reid, c Johnson, b Biggar I.	3
Moore, c Cooper, b Biggar I.	1
Dobson, b Biggar I.	0
Nutter, c Moore, b Biard	4
Willis, c McWhinney, b Baird	0
Whitehead, not out	4
Seal, b Biggar I.	0
Skinner, b Baird	2
Heath, c McWhinney, b Baird.	0
Byes	1
Total	38

TORONTO, 2nd Innings.	
Heath, c and b Biggar II.	0
Skinner, c and b Palmer mi.	0
Seal, b Biggar II.	0
Whitehead, c Johnston, b Mc-Whinney	10
Willis, c Palmer mi., b McWhinney	3
Nutter, s McWhinney	0
Dobson, s McWhinney	0
Moore, b Biggar I.	2
Reid, l b w Baird	7
Stockdale, c Moore, b McWhinney	0
Baxter, c Moore, b Baird	3
Robinson, not out	1
Total	26

IIND'S, 1st Inning.	
Biggar II., run out	14
Moore, c Stockdale, b Whitehead	9
Baird, b Robinson	43
Norsworthy, b Robinson	16
Biggar I., c Baxter, b Robinson	0
Palmer mi., c Reid, b Robinson	0
Johnston II., b Baxter	0
Palmer ma., c and b Robinson.	3
Cooper, not out	3
Douglas, b Baxter	1
MacWhinney	8
Wide balls	5
Total	102

IIND'S, 2nd Innings	
Cooper, b Baxter	1
Douglas, c Seal, b Dobson	6
Johnson II., b Baxter	6
Biggar I., c and b Nutter	2
McWhinney, b Dobson	0
Palmer mi., run out	10
Palmer ma., c and b Dobson	0
Moore, c Baxter, b Dobson	0
Biggar II., not out	4
Norsworthy, not out	6
Baird, did not bat	
Wide balls	1
Total	38

LAKE LODGE I. vs. RIDLEY II.

The return game was played at Grimsby on Wednesday, June 11th, and in a very low scoring game, Ridley succeeded in winning. Biggar I. and Soanes bowled well for Ridley, while Watkins and Phin did all the bowling for Lake Lodge.

.. LAKE LODGE, 1st Innings	
Andrews, b Biggar I.	2
Brown, c Snyder, b Soanes	10
Watkins, c Bright, b Soanes	5
Phin, b Biggar I.	0
Morris ma., c Hyslop, b Soanes	1
Stock, c Douglas, b Soanes	0
Morris mi., c Douglas, b Biggar I.	0

Peene, b Biggar I.	0
Whitelaw, c Douglas, b Soanes.	2
Scarlett, not out	0
Atkins, c Douglas, b Biggar I.	0
Extras	1
Total	21

RIDLEY, 1st Innings		RIDLEY, 2nd Innings.	
Osborne, c and b Watkins	0	Douglas, c Stock, b Watkins...	5
Bright ma., c Whitelaw, b Phin	10	Osborne, l b w Phin	2
Soanes, b Phin	4	Bright ma., not out	11
Hyslop, b Phin	6	Soanes, b Phin	5
Rogers, b Watkins	8	Hyslop, not out	12
Biggar I., b Phin	2	Rogers	
Greening ma., c Watkins, b Phin	0	Biggar I.	
Cooper, c Scarlett, b Watkins..	0	Greening ma.	
Snyder, c Morris ma., b Watkins	0	Cooper	
Douglas, not out	0	Snyder	
Thompson, b Phin	1	Thompson	
		Extras	2
Total	31	Total	37

U. C. C. II. vs. RIDLEY II.

While our first team played U. C. C. I., our second eleven was busy with U. C. C. II., and managed to win by a comfortable margin.

U. C. C. batted first and were all out for 34 runs, owing to good bowling by Rogers and Biggar II.

Ridley then went in and ran up the good score of 162 for 8 wickets. Rogers 31, Bright ma. 30 (resigned), Osborne 22, not out, Norsworthy 19, Soanes 18, Bright mi. 13, being those to reach double figures.

U. C. C. II.		RIDLEY II.	
Hargraft, c Moore, b Biggar II.	7	Stringer, b Mulqueen	6
Thompson, b Rogers	4	Biggar II., run out	2
Huckvale, b Biggar II.	0	Bright mi., c Granger, b Mulqueen	13
Wilson, b Rogers	0		
Hyland, b Biggar II.	0	Moore, l b w Hargraft	6
Davis, b Rogers	0	Soanes, c Hargraft, b Thompson	18
Mulqueen, c MacWhinney, b Biggar II.	2	Norsworthy, b Hargraft	19
		Rogers, c and b Hargraft	31
Babbit, c Osborne, b Rogers...	4	Bright ma., resigned	30
Granger, c Soanes, b MacWhinney	7	Hyslop, b Hargraft	3
		Osborne, resigned	22
Drynam, c Bright ma., b Biggar II.	0	MacWhinney, resigned	4
Hamilton, not out	6	Extras	8
Extras	4		
Total	34	Total	162

LAKE LODGE vs. RIDLEY III.

On Wednesday, June 4, Lake Lodge motored from Grimsby to play Ridley III., and succeeded in winning rather easily, owing to the excellent batting of Watkins (44). Ridley were able to make but 49, Hyslop (11) being high, while Lake Lodge's total reached 75.

Watkins and Phin bowled well for the visitors, while Biggar pri. and Biggar sec. between them got all the wickets for Ridley.

LAKE LODGE		RIDLEY III.	
Watkins, c Hyslop, b Couch ...	44	Biggar II., c Stock b Phin	0
Andrews, b Biggar II.	3	Osborne, l b w Watkins	6
Brown, c Johnson, b Biggar II..	7	Moore, c Watkins, b Phin.....	9
Phin, c Hyslop, b Biggar II....	8	Norsworthy, c Morris, b Watkins	1
Morris ma., b Biggar II.......	0	Biggar I., c Peene, b Phin	1
Stock, c Hyslop, b Biggar I....	10	Couch, c Stock, b Phin........	5
Whitelaw, b Biggar I.	2	Hyslop, b Phin	11
Morris mi., c Gordon, b Biggar II.	0	Gordon I., b Phin	7
McGivern, b Biggar II.	1	Johnston II., c Phin, b Andrews	2
Scarlett, c Gordon, b Biggar II.	0	Palmer ma., not out	3
Peene, not out	0	Bright ma., b Andrews.......	1
		Extras	3
Total	75	Total	49

APPLEBY I. vs. RIDLEY III.

On Wednesday, June 11th, Appleby I. played our third eleven at Ridley, and in a two-innings game were defeated by a small number of runs. Appleby batted first and were all out for 47, of which Hutchinson got 24 and Allan 17.

Ridley did a little better and managed to gather 51 runs in the first innings, Biggar II. (10) being the only one in double figures.

Both teams did better in the second innings, Appleby making 97 for 8, and drawing, while Ridley made 102 for 7. Northy did well for Appleby, with 41, while McWhinney, Biggar II. and Goldie did good work for Ridley.

RIDLEY III., 1st Innings		RIDLEY III., 2nd Innings	
Biggar II., c Moss, b Gillard....	10	Biggar II., c Moss, b Wadsworth	18
Goldie, b Gillard	5	Palmer mi., c Thomson, b Wads-	
Phin, b Northy	5	worth	5
Couch, c Boughner, b Gillard..	6	McWhinney, run out	19
McWhinney, b Northy	9	Couch, run out	0
Bright mi., run out	1	Goldie, b Northy	28
Johnston II., c Thomas, b Wads-		Phin, c Allan, b Northy	4
worth	4	Johnston II., run out	10
Gordon I., b Northy	1	Palmer ma., not out	0
Palmer ma., b Wadsworth.....	3	Bright mi., not out	
Palmer mi., not out	0	Gledhill } Did not bat	
Gledhill, c Moss, b Wadsworth..	1	Gordon I.	
Extras	6	Extras	16
Total	51	7 for	102

APPLEBY I., 1st Innings		APPLEBY I., 2nd Innings	
Wadsworth, b Gordon I.	1	Wadsworth, b Palmer mi.......	5
Thomson, c Gordon I., b Palmer		Thomson, c Couch, b Palmer mi.	5
mi.	0	Gillard, c and b Gordon.......	6
Rechnitzer, b Gordon I.	1	Hutchinson II., c Phin, b Big-	
Moss, run out	2	gar II.	13
Northy, c Phin, b Gordon I.....	24	Northy, b Gledhill	41
Hutchinson I., b Couch........	24	Hutchinson II., b Biggar II.....	0
Allan, c Biggar, b McWhinney.	17	Allan, b Biggar II.	8
Webster, b McWhinney........	0	Moss, not out	9
Gillard, not out	0	Webster, b Couch	3
Hutchinson II., b McWhinney..	0	Rechnitzer, not out	6
Boughner, c Gordon, b McWhin-		Boughner, did not bat	
ney	0	Extras	1
Extras	1		
Total	47	8 for	97

Dean's House

DEAN'S HOUSE vs. APPLEBY II.

s House Eleven visited Appleby School early in
i very enjoyable outing.
itted first, but did not do very well, and the side
s than 50, on a good wicket.
use did much better and Bright mi. himself made
i the whole Appleby team, the total being 108, of
also made doubles.
game refreshments were served, and all voted the
ccess.
tely, press of work prevented a return game, which
s good work well deserved.
, the Dean's House is to be congratulated on the
et spirit developed, and we shall expect several of
make places on the first net next year.
hes were played during the season against the
the first a very close game indeed, was won by only

t match was played on the last afternoon of term,
am pitch was turned over to the two young teams
ant match.
ood game resulted, in which Dean's House, thanks
l Bongard, were again the victors.
vho played on the Dean's House team were as fol-
i., Palmer mi., Gledhill (against Appleby), Coun-
nk, Wilson, Warren, Osler mi., Cliff ma., Cliff mi.,
tto, Shurley, Eakens, Eliot, Stewart, Gordon mi.,

Bowled

Our Wicket Keeper

THE LOWER SCHOOL

IN all the history of the School, there can hardly be found records of a more trying and difficult year than the one which has just closed, and that the last term of it should have been so successful must be a source of considerable satisfaction to the staff and parents as well as to the boys themselves.

With the arrival of the influenza epidemic in the early Fall, work was only carried on under the greatest difficulties, games and physical development were merely nominal, and the whole period held nothing but worry and anxiety for everyone.

Even after Christmas the tension was very great and the long, tedious wait for the cold weather with its attendant, skating, added considerably to the difficulties. The opening of the Summer term brought little or no relief; the weather was cold and wet; out-of-door amusements were almost impossible, and everybody was gradually sinking to the depths of despair. The whole holiday, May 24th, celebrated in beautiful weather, cheered up every one, however, and since then the usual events have come and gone in rapid succession, always helped on by beautiful weather, and everybody has been able to enjoy them to the fullest extent.

Throughout the year the School has been filled to its utmost capacity; except for the "flu," the health record could hardly have been better. Progress has been as good as ever and the few games we have been able to play have brought us a large percentage of victories.

Once more the time has come round when we must say "good-bye" to many old friends. Altogether, about twenty boys hope to move on to the Upper School, and many of them are quite old-timers.

They may be sure that we shall miss them considerably, and to all we wish the very best of good luck. Their places will be filled by others and we shall "carry on" in the same old way, but the many little attentions they have shown us will live on after them, and we trust that their interest in us, in the future, will be no less than it has been in the past. When they return in September they will begin an entirely new chapter and no doubt will require a little time to get used to their new surroundings. To any who may be a little doubtful, may we suggest that many others have had to do the same thing before them, and that the time will soon come when they will be able to look back with satisfaction and perhaps, too, give a helping hand to some other "new kid." Of the twenty vacancies thus created, many have already been filled and applications are coming in rapidly. With the same staff returning in September, we have every reason therefore to look forward with pleasure to the coming year and to hope that it will be as happy, as successful and as progressive as the past ones have been.

CRICKET

Lennox was elected Captain, with Grobba as the next man, and, although prospects at first were not very good, everybody worked well and it was soon apparent that there were some very promising players in the School.

Although bowlers were scarce, Lennox and Grobba proved themselves quite capable of giving all the service necessary, and it was mainly due to their excellent work that so many victories were gained. Their contest for the bowling prize was indeed quite the event of the season, Lennox (4.32) being successful by only .05 of a run.

In the batting Macdonald (8.06) proved himself to be the best run-getter and was very useful on several occasions, but Lennox (7.75) and Millidge (7.09) gave him a close run.

The fielding throughout the season was quite good, and although the prize was awarded to McCormack, who worked very hard and was always in the right place at the right time, Millidge, with fifteen catches to his credit, did excellent work and deserves a prize almost as much.

A good deal of care was taken in selecting the team for each game, and this caused much keenness, but results proved that the decisions were well taken, and it added considerably to the enthusiasm of the candidates. Fourteen boys were given a place in a School game, five of them playing in every one.

Colours were awarded to Macdonald, Millidge, Barnet, Grobba, Coddington, Hartt, Case, Baird, McCormack, DeWitt and Hislop ma.

RECORD

May 28—At home, Ridley 35 and 31, Lake Lodge 46 and 30 (for 8), lost.

May 31—At home, Ridley 14 and 54, Appleby 33 and 35, tied.

June 7—At home, Ridley 42 and 77, U. C. C. 27, won.

June 11—At Oakville, Ridley 29 and 66, Appleby 38 and 17, won.

June 14—At Toronto, Ridley 41, U. C. C. 30, won.

June 18—At Grimsby, Ridley 17 and 37, Lake Lodge 41 and 6 (for 5), lost.

For the first game of the season, and the first of any kind

played this year, the Lake Lodge boys were our visitors. Ridley batted first and "poking" was the order of the day, and the wickets fell in rapid succession. Lennox was the only one to show any real form, and with 20 not out, out of a total of 35, did his best to pull his team out of the hole.

Lake Lodge replied with 41, Stock and Marshall being the only two to make any headway against the bowling of Lennox and Grobba (12 for 25).

In the second innings Macdonald (11) did his best to save the game, but getting no support, we could only make 31, thus leaving Lake Lodge 20 to get to win, a task they accomplished for the loss of 8 wickets.

The second game was against Appleby School and proved to be the most exciting game one could wish to see. Appleby batted first and through good cricket by Bloomfield I. put together a total of 33. Ridley went to the wicket with the best intentions, but the Bloomfield brothers had everything their own way, and the innings closed for a miserable 14.

In their second attempt, Appleby put together another 36, leaving us to get 56 to win and 45 minutes in which to do it.

Grobba (9) and Hartt (8) helped things along considerably, but to Coddington (not out, 13) went the honour of the day. Run by run he pushed up the score towards the required number until, just as we had equalled our opponents' score, Hislop ma., the last wicket, was run out.

In the intense excitement of the last ten minutes, the scorers lost the count for a moment, and so with the victory possible to either side it was only fair to count it as a tied game. Grobba again headed the bowling with 12 wickets for 19 runs.

The last game at home was against U. C. C. and ended in our first victory.

In the second innings Macdonald (30) showed splendid form and Coddington (11) again made himself a nuisance to the bowlers, whilst Lennox added 8 more to bring the total up to 77. Time being then too short for the U.C.C. boys to bat again, Ridley won on the first innings.

For the first game away, the team went to Oakville and spent a delightful day. Ridley again batted first, Macdonald (8) and Millidge (8) being the best scorers in a total of 29, to which Appleby responded with 33. In the second innings disaster stared us in the face, for at the lunch interval eight f our wickets had fallen for 17 runs—only 13 ahead of the Appleby score for one innings. After lunch, however, Millidge came to the rescue with

LOWER SCHOOL SNAPS

a splendidly played 26 not out, Hartt (15) giving him good assistance and the innings closed for 66.

Requiring 57 to win, Appleby started out in good style to
play out time and so win on the first innings. Lennox (5 wickets
for 8), and Grobba (5 for 9) were equally determined, and all
their wickets fell for 17 after an innings of nearly 1½ hours.

For the second game away, we had our annual boat trip to
Toronto, and everybody enjoyed a very happy day. The sun was
intensely hot, in spite of the early start, and the trip across the
lake was all that could be desired. For the third time in succession, Ridley batted first, on a very soft and difficult pitch. The
first two wickets fell for no score, but Millidge (13) again came
to the rescue and Lennox (8), Grobba (8) and McCormack (6
not out) brought the total to 41.

In the first part of the U.C.C. innings, everything went our
way, their first six wickets falling for 7 runs. Seagram (20, not
out), made a determined effort to win the game, but with Lennox
at his best and Grobba improving at every ball, they were all out
for 30.

In the second innings Ridley had scored 13 for the loss of one
wicket when heavy rain put an end to the game, thereby giving
us our third victory. After a swim and ice cream galore, we drove
back to the boat, and had another delightful trip across the lake,
arriving home just in time to avoid study.

The last game of the season was played at Grimsby, where
our spell of good fortune was broken.

Going to the wickets first, Macdonald (8) and Lennox (5 not
out) were the only two to give any account of themselves, eight
of the rest being caught without scoring.

Through poor fielding, Lake Lodge were able to put together
a total of 41, Lennox capturing six of the ten wickets for 16 runs.

In the second innings matters improved a little, Millidge (8)
and Lennox (8) being top scorers, and the total reached 37, thus
leaving Lake Lodge 14 to get to save defeat, with only a few
minutes of play left.

Lennox (2 for 5) and Grobba (3 for 1) got to work quickly
and with a little more time could possibly have won the game, as
five of the Lake Lodge men had been despatched for 6 runs, and
all of their best bats were out.

In the Dormitory Games No. II., Capt. Grobba, had no trou-
ble in winning the series and so deprived No. III. of the flag, which
was demanded with considerable force and carried downstairs
in triumph.

CROSS COUNTRY

The Cross Country Race, postponed in the Fall on account of the "flu," was run on May 15th, and attracted more attention than ever.

Every boy (53) who was allowed to line up for the start, and every body who started finished in the alloted time.

Case (aged 11) arrived home first in good time, and so won the Reid Cup and Silver Medal, whilst the bronze goes to Grant (aged 10) who came up just ahead of Gray (aged 14).

The masters' cakes, given to the first boy home in each dormitory, were won by Gray, No. II., Hislop ma., No. IV., Neeve, No. I., Kinnear, No. III., and Wismer, No. IV. The full returns, in the order in which the boys finished, are as follows:

Case, Grant, Gray, Hislop ma., Neeve, Millidge, Davies, Kinnear, Wismer, Mather, Biggar, Baird, Barnet, Hislop mi., Thamson, Macy, Cronyn, Stringer mi., Dafoe, Robins, Coddington, Newman, Lennox, McCormack, Innes, Rogers, Fairbank, Shell, Crombie, Brent, Mitchell, Hartt, Ingalls mi., Yates, Willan, Botterell, Arnott, Stringer ma., Grobba, Powell, Weatherston, Ingalls ma., Robertson, Henderson, Harrison, Waters, Chapple, Gates, McBean mi., Ridout, McBean ma., Platt, Howell. Time, 11.17.

Military Drill has been carried on as usual and a good deal of useful work was done early in the year.

During the recent exceptionally hot weather, however, enthusiasm waned considerably and the proficiency of each section suffered a good deal.

The standard reached in the Company Drill was quite as high as that of last year, more work having been done.

Lennox was appointed Commanding Officer and during the year has learned to handle his men with considerable success.

In the contest for the Taylor Shield, for which Col. Thairs acts as judge, No. I. under Mather, and No. III. under Botterell, tied for first place, No. I. gaining on odd point in the extra three minutes' test. No. IV. under Macdonald, came third, and No. II. under Gray, last. After the inspection ice cream was served on the field, and everybody was greatly relieved that the much-dreaded day was over.

Sports Day, May 30th, brought with it beautiful weather, many visitors and much enjoyment to everybody. The sensation of the day was the winning of the Goodr* ham Championship Shield by Fairbank, by one point, from Hislop ma.

During the year many boys have devoted a good deal of time and interest in collecting school pictures, but only six books were entered for the Photograph Album Competition. Of these Arnott's was selected as the best, but Brent's and Water's both deserve a great deal of credit and their albums will be a source of considerable pleasure and pride to them for many years to come.

About 150 pictures were taken, from which just under 3,000 prints were ordered.

The past year has seen the institution of what is hoped will be an annual swimming contest. The different events were decided during the last week of the term and proved to be very popular . Gray had no difficulty in winning the Senior Championship, whilst the Junior was won by Case, with Innes a close second. The fololwing was the programme:

Two lengths—Senior, Gray; junior, Case.
One length—Senior, Gray; junior, Case.
One length on the back—Senior, Ridout; junior, Case.
Long plunge—Senior, Ridout; junior, Biggar.
Front dive—Senior, Dafoe; junior, Case.
Back dive—Senior, Gray and Botterell; junior, Innes.
1st voluntary dive—Senior, Gray; junior, Innes.
2nd voluntary dive—Senior, Gray and Ridout; junior, Innes.

During the last month we have been glad to welcome back two of our old masters, Mr. Brock from the Base Hospital at Calais, and Mr. Hern from Siberia.

Mrs. Burnett also paid us a visit on the first day of term, and left behind her a small nephew.

The Dormitory Tidiness Competition goes to No. II., with No. V. coming a close second and ice cream on the front door steps was much enjoyed by everybody on the last day of term.

The Punctuality Prize was won by Arnott, who succeeded in getting through the year without a single late.

Mrs. Baird's General Tidiness Prize goes to the boy whose personal belongings and appearance are best cared for, was given to McCormack, who just missed-winning it last year.

In the Dormitory Championship, each dormitory won one event, the soccer games not being played, and so No. III. (Lennox) claims the cup by virtue of having won the most games.

During the term a very handsome contribution of about $50 worth of books for the Library was received from Mrs. Fairbank, every one of which has already given a great deal of pleasure to many boys. This is Mrs. Fairbank's second contribution to the Lower School this year, and her generosity and interest is fully appreciated by all.

Another much appreciated kindness shown to us during the year is the promise by the Winnipeg parents of a cup for the Dormitory Games, whilst from Mr. W. S. Greening has come a request to present an annual prize for general knowledge.

Reading Contest

About the middle of the term the annual reading contest was held. The entries this year exceeded those of former years and only by the elimination process were the judges able to choose those boys who entered the finals. A splendid spirit was evident in each form, where nearly all took part in the contest. MacMahon, Stringer ma. and Osborne were left in the finals, Osborne winning out, closely followed in points by Stringer ma. and MacMahon.

Shooting Competition

The usual competition was held during June, and with Sergt. Gellately in charge, some good scores were made.

The following cadets qualified for the final shoot: Mosher, Shearson, Biggar II., Osler ma., Baker, Bertram, MacWhinney, Goldie, Turnbull, Kertland, O'Brian.

In the final event, Bertram won out, with O'Brian and Turnbull tie for second. To break the tie, the latter pair shot again, and O'Brian made one point more than his younger adversary.

Dean's House Library

During the "flu" epidemic, nearly all the books in the Dean's House Library were given to the sick boys in the Hospital, and in consequence we are facing a new year with very depleted book shelves. Any contribution of books which can be spared will be most gratefully received by Mr. Powell; and may be sent to him at any time.

Congratulations to Wallace ma., MacDonell and Olmsted, who were successful in the recent R. M. C. examinations.

Styles in Straws at Ridley

A Memorial Service for Old Ridleians

who gave their lives in the war

June 22nd, 1919

FORM OF SERVICE

PROCESSIONAL HYMN . . . . No. 380
           COLLEGE CHOIR

SPECIAL PSALMS . . . . 23 and 121

FIRST LESSON . . . . Isaiah xl. 1-11
           CADET STRINGER ma.

HYMN (instead of Magnificat) "God of Our Fathers" . . . . No. 358

SECOND LESSON . . . . Rev. vii v. 17
           CADET OSBORNE

NUNC DIMITTIS. . . . .

HYMN . . . . "O Valiant Hearts"

ADDRESS . . . .
           THE PRINCIPAL

OFFERTORY . . . . "Abide With Me"
           CAPT. LEONARD BISHOP

SPECIAL MEMORIAL PRAYERS. . . . .

"LAST POST" . . . .
           CADET WILLIAMS

HYMN (to be sung kneeling) "Sleep Thy Last Sleep" . . . . . No. 282

FUNERAL MARCH . . . .
           MR. W. T. THOMPSON

RECESSIONAL HYMN, "For All the Saints" . . . . No. 219

PRINCIPAL'S ADDRESS

WE are met today to do honour to the memory of our glorious dead. From time to time, as one by one they have fallen on the battlefield, passing on the torch to those who succeeded them, we have commemorated their individual achievements and sacrifice; we have thanked God that they met the supreme test and were not found wanting, and have asked Him to fill the hearts of their sorrowing loved ones with the Divine consolation.

To-day our purpose is somewhat different. As we sit here quietly in God's house, we desire to recall them vividly to our remembrance, and to enter into communion with them. To-day we want to look at these sixty heroic souls in the mass, as a company, just as we might look upon our Cadet Corps, to which they once belonged, drawn up for inspection. If you can imagine them standing before us in serried ranks, eager to spring to action at the commander's voice, animated by a single purpose, moving as a single living force, unterrified, confident, resolute to achieve, you will begin to understand the power of their unified spirit, and the tremendous spiritual energy that they have bequeathed to us, and to this beloved land in which we dwell. Are we worthy of this bequest? Are we capable of putting it to its intended use?

What is the intended use of this spiritual power of the group, which is like the power of confined waters ready to fall with immense impact upon the assembled turbines for the release of mass energy and the creation of light to lighten up the dark places of the earth, and by its radiance to dissipate evil? As it was the purpose of our men when they went to war to fight against a great and threatening power of evil, so it is the purpose of this grouped spiritual power bequeathed to us through the sacrifice of these heroic lives that we should bind ourselves into a fighting force to strive against the kingdom of evil in our midst.

What is this kingdom of evil? When those of us who are no longer young were children, the kingdom of evil was represented in our minds by the terrible Satanic individuality of the Devil, who went roaming up and down the world seeking whom he might devour; little children, those who had grown aged and strong men and women who knew not God. All sin was personal and all evil individual.

But in our day we have come to recognize more clearly than

did former generations that a large part of the evil of the world is super-personal, and must be charged against the group, the community, the nation. It becomes characteristic of the mass, and infects, with some exceptions, the individuals within the group. We may place different constructions upon the terms "original sin" and "the natural depravity of the human heart," but common sense teaches us that many sins are bred in us by infection, from the environment in which we are born, and brought up, and in which we carry on the activities of our lives.

Let us glance for a moment at a few of those super-personal sins which constitute the kingdom of evil, against which the spirit of our dead bids us marshall our forces and arms us to fight for the Kingdom of God.

1. The Spirit of Militarism. This is the spirit which made the world-wide war possible, which spilt the blood of those we think of to-day, as it did of many millions of others, innocent of any criminal intent. Up to this time this spirit has been, throughout the world's history, the supreme national spirit of evil. It was the military power that arrested Jesus, stripped Him, beat Him with leaded thongs, pressed into His brow the wreath of thorns and drove the spikes through His hands and feet. We may hope and pray that the ocean of blood shed in this war has quenched that evil spirit; but it is not really so. It will lift its head again. The spirit of our dead calls to us to strive against that evil spirit as one of the chief citadels of the kingdom of evil.

2. The Mob Spirit. The mob spirit as we ordinarily understand it is the social spirit gone mad. The social spirit acts so powerfully upon individuals when the restraints of self-control are withdrawn that the crowd becomes drunk on its own emotions. At the present time the mob spirit is the most dangerous of the powers of evil in almost every land. We usually associate it only with the labouring class. But this is a great mistake. It may break out among trained and disciplined troops. It may show itself in a great university, or even among school children. It may be found among associations of leaders of industry and combinations of capitalists. It is present wherever the deliberations of any group of men are controlled by passion and the determination to conquer at any price. It was the mob spirit that shouted for the release of Barabbas and for the crucifixion of Jesus. It is Hell let loose for assault upon the Kingdom of God.

3. The Spirit of Covetousness. Greed of gain is in the beginning an individual passion. But it becomes a super-personal spirit when it animates a group of men who combine for the

exploitation of men or of natural wealth. It is one of the great
evils of our day and one of the prime causes of the unrest that
seems at times to threaten revolution. The group spirit of the
money-changers who obtained a footing in the temple courts was
one of the causes that led to the arrest and death of Jesus.

4. The Spirit of Ostentation. Another evil spirit that is
abroad, twin-sister of Greed, and breeds bitterness and hatred,
and threatens worse, is the spirit of ostentation, or the vulgar
display of wealth, coupled with the insatiable craving for pleasure.
It becomes super-personal when it is dignified by the name of the
Fashion, for only the very strong-minded—the remnant—can resist the fashion, which wields an immense influence over the
majority. This evil spirit engenders class pride and its obverse,
class contempt. These are the negation of the solidarity and
Christian love of the brotherhood. They are the denial of human
fraternity. When Jesus was nailed to the tree He bore in a de-
graded form of death that contempt for the lower classes which
de-humanized the upper classes of His day.

5. Selfishness. A clear understanding of the teaching of
Jesus and the purpose of His life leads us to appreciate the meaning of sin. Reduced to its simplest terms, sin is selfishness. To
be in a state of sin is to be rooted in self. It is the all-pervading
weakness of mortal nature from which no one is exempt. It becomes a super-personal spirit when it embraces the group, the
community, the nation. We have seen it on the grand scale in
the slave traffic, the opium traffic, the Congo rubber traffic, col-
onial exploitation, and in a thousand other forms. We have seen
it at the Peace Conference; we see it everywhere. We feel its
effects in every department of human activity, and in every walk
of life. It was this spirit that paralyzed the work of Jesus and
prevented the coming of the Kingdom of God during His life-time.

How are we to fight against these evil spirits that afflict
humanity and hide from us the face of God? This is the great
social problem of the Church of Christ. This is the real problem
of social service, namely, to develop a super-personal spirit of
righteousness, of brotherhood, of good-will, to resist, to attack,
to overthrow and cast out these evil spirits that resist the coming
of the Kingdom of God.

For you and for me, as we are met here today, to renew our
memory of the achievements, the self-denial, the self-renuncia-
tion and sacrifice of our little company of sixty, for the most part
in the first blush of manhood, we realize that there has been
created and released for our help and use a corporate, God-like

LOWER SCHOOL SNAPS

spirit that has the power in our struggle against sin to make our strength as the strength of ten. Take the single instance of the spirit of unselfishness that they have bequeathed for our appropriation. It was no part of their obedience as soldiers. It was not laid down in the soldier's hand-book. It was never promulgated in general orders. It was never urged by any captain or platoon commander, and yet this Christ-like quality of unselfishness was universal throughout our armies. It pervaded all ranks and all grades of the service. Many a cross on the battlefield marks the deliberate sacrifice of a life that some other might be saved.

The symbols of the corporate spirit that our beloved dead have left us are the poppy-lighted crosses of France and Flanders. The men who fought and bled and died there have redeemed us with a price that we cannot yet begin to estimate . We shall never be able to reckon its full total. In all the world's history there has been no redemption from evil without suffering and sacrifice, and the shedding of innocent blood, and this redemption only typifies for us the great world redemption won for us by the Cross of Christ.

Try to conceive once more that little company of sixty souls, as a unified spirit, almost for us at this moment a corporeal presence. As we sit here in God's house can we not feel that presence? Can we not feel that spirit brooding over us? Can we not feel it filling our hearts? Can we not realize it as a holy inspiration? If we can, then the spirit of our dead is a sword placed in our hands. It is a shield for our protection when we are in danger of assault. We can feel that protection as did our sorely harried troops at Mons who thought they saw God's angels in the sky.

> "The silent legions of the Lord
>   Came riding by—
> The blinding flash of the flaming sword
>   Under the flaming sky.
>
> A handful passed from the jaws of death
>   And stumbled by,
> But a host was quelled by a fiery Breath
>   Under the flaming sky."

And now look once more at those sixty heroic souls, drawn up so that we may see each one and recognize his features. Pick out the one you loved best, purged now of all earthly dross. Think of his qualities—the honest face, the fearless eyes, the brave and loving heart, the open hand, the attitude of willing service. Can we think of these things without making a solemn vow of consecration of our own lives to follow in their footsteps? Can we hesitate to consecrate ourselves, our souls and bodies, as they did, to the service of our fellow-men! I think not.

We cannot conclude this memorial of our heroic dead without a word of sympathy to their parents and relatives. It is hard to give that sympathy any fitting expression, but we wish them to know that their grief is our grief, and that we claim a part in their sorrow, just as we claim a part in the pride and glory that is theirs through what their beloved ones have done for us. And so we say to them in the words of a Canadian poet:

"Not in the horns and trumpets—but e'en as the mourners kneel,
Thus shall a nation whisper: Know ye the pride we feel,
Ye who have paid our ransom, paid it in blood and tears,
Your sons have brought us freedom. Look! They have changed
    the years.
And the thing they have brought us is finer than palace, or jewels,
    or gold;
The right of the weak to flourish, as the strong have flourished of
    old.
Ye,—ye have sown in your tears that a world may reap in its joy,
Ye also have cleansed the years . . . with the life of your boy."

Upon the monumental crosses that mark the graves in France and Flanders are to be carved the words: "Their name liveth for evermore." That is a splendid sentence, a fitting sentiment for the passer-by. But we can offer to every parent who mourns for a son, a message of greater comfort and of deeper assurance. To such a parent we can say with profound conviction, in the words of the Captain of our salvation: "Go thy way; thy son LIVETH."

"O VALIANT HEARTS"

O valiant hearts, who to your glory came,
Through dust of conflict and through battle flame;
Tranquil you lie, your knightly virtue proved,
Your memory hallowed in the land you loved.

Proudly you gathered, rank on rank to war,
As who heard God's message from afar;
All you had hoped for, all you had, you gave
To save mankind—yourselves you scorned to save.

Long years ago, as earth lay dark and still,
Rose a loud cry upon a lonely hill,
While in the frailty of our human clay
Christ, our Redeemer, passed the self-same way.

Still stands His Cross from that dread hour to this
Like some bright star above the dark abyss;
Still, through the veil, the victor's pitying eyes
Look down to bless our lesser calvaries.

These were His servants, in His steps they trod
Following through death the maryr'd Son of God:
Victor He rose; victorious too shall rise
They who have drunk His cup of sacrifice.

O risen Lord, O Shepherd of our dead,
Whose Cross has brought them and whose Staff has led—
In glorious hope their proud and sorrowing land
Commits her children to thy gracious hand.—Amen.
—John Arkwright.

SPECIAL PRAYERS

FOR THOSE WHO MOURN

Almighty God, with whom do live the spirits of those who depart hence in the Lord, and who hast taught us not to be sorry as men without the hope for those who have laid down their lives for the sake of their brethren, and for the good of thy kingdom, we pray that thou will comfort those who mourn their loved ones who counted not the cost, but yielded their lives gladly, in the great cause. Pour into their hearts thy deep consolation; help them to feel the pride, which is our glory, that their dear ones were worthy in the day of trial. Bring them out of their great tribulation into the peace that passeth understanding. We ask it through Him who gave His life for us all, Jesus Christ our Lord. Amen.

DEDICATORY PRAYER

O Lord our Heavenly Father who art always ready to listen to thy children and to receive them when they approach thee, we thank thee that thou hast accepted these of our number, slain in battle, whom we have committed to thy gracious keeping for more glorious service in the state to which thou hast called them. And here, following their example, we offer and present unto thee, O Lord, our souls and bodies, a living sacrifice, for the good of our fellow men and for the increase of thy kingdom upon earth. To-day we offer thee anew this pledge as a fitting memorial of those who have fought the good fight, and kept the faith, and have gone before us to their reward. Lest we forget, renew within us day by day, the spirit of our Lord and Saviour, Jesus Christ. Amen.

IN MEMORIAM

O merciful God, the Father of our Lord Jesus Christ, who is the resurrection and the life; in whom whosoever liveth and believeth in him shall not die eternally: We bless thy holy name for these thy servants, once members of this college, departed this life in thy faith and fear; beseeching thee to give us grace so to follow their good examples that with them we may be partakers of thy heavenly kingdom. Grant this, O Father, for Jesus Christ's sake. Amen.

"I heard a voice from heaven, saying unto me: Write: From henceforth blessed are the dead which die in the Lord: Even so saith the spirit, for they rest from their labours."

"Last Post," Cadet Williams.

Hymn (to be sung kneeling) No. 282, "Sleep Thy Last Sleep."

Funeral March.

Benediction.

CANADAM MORIENTES RECREARUNT

GORDON, Capt. W. L. L., 2nd Bn., April 23rd, 1915.
JARVIS, Lieut. W. D. P., 3rd Bn., April 24, 1915.
MACKENZIE, Lieut. G. A. G., 16th Bn., May 23rd, 1915.
NOXON, Lieut. G. C., Royal Grens., October 1st, 1915.
CHESTNUT, Lieut. J. A., 35th Batt., R.F.A., December 19th, 1915.
GRAVES, Lieut. T. M., 76th Punjabis, April 22nd, 1916.
GRASETT, Lieut. H. H., June 2nd, 1916.
BOURNE, Lieut. H. H., June 2nd, 1916.
ZIEGLER, Lieut. E. H., June 7th, 1916.
WILSON, Lieut. H. M., 15th Bn., June 7, 1916.
VAN-DER-SMISSEN, Capt. W. H. V., 3rd Bn., June 13th, 1916.
DOBSON, Major W. J., 1st Bn., July 6th, 1916.
BLAKE, Capt. G. E., Oxford and Bucks L. I., July 23rd, 1916.
WRONG, Lieut. H. V., 15th Bn. (Lanc. Fus.), July, 1916 .
DICKSON, Pte. C. B., C.M.R., August 18th, 1916.
NORTON-TAYLOR, Lieut. W. H., 21st Bn., September 16, 1916.
INGERSOLL, Lieut. J. H., Lincolns and R.A.F., September 16, 1916.
MORTON, Lieut. B. A. E., 75th Bn., September 24, 1916.
WADSWORTH, Lieut. D. R., 75th Bn., October 13th, 1916.
NORSWORTHY, Lieut. A. J., 73rd Bn., October 13th, 1916.
FATT, Lieut. W. M., 50th Bn. and R.F.C., January 4th, 1917.
MANLEY, Lieut. J. F., 72nd Bn., April 15th, 1917.
JONES, Major R. W. F., April 15th, 1917.
PORTER, A. A., American Ambul. Corps., April 27th, 1917.
TRIMMER, Capt. A. S., M.C. and Bar, 10th Bn., May 4th, 1917.
HART, Gr. J. L., 54th Batty., May 7th, 1917.
WAINWRIGHT, Gr. J., 54th Batty., May 8th, 1917.
JARDINE, Lieut. G., R.F.C., July 20th, 1917.
GATES, Lieut. A. F., R.F.A., August 8th, 1917.
SIMS, Lieut. D. C., R.F.A., August 8th, 1917.
MONTGOMERY, Lieut. C. C. S., R.F.C., August 14th, 1917.
SPENCE, Major F. R., 2nd Bn., August 18th, 1917.
McLEA, Lieut. K. W., 3rd Div., C.F.A., October 28th, 1917.
SCOTT, Lieut. J. G., R.N.A.S., Jan. 13th, 1918.
BOYD, Lieut. H. C., K.O.Y.L.I. Feb. 15th, 1918.
SHAW-WOOD, Lieut. R., R.F.C., Mar. 20th, 1918.
CARPENTER, Lieut. Chas. R.F.A., March, 1918.
TRENCH, Sergt. Archer, 71st Batty., C.F.A., June 3rd, 1918.
NIEGHORN, 2nd Lieut. C., R.A.F., June, 1918.
BARWICK, Lt. R. L., R.A.F., July 5th, 1918.
WOODRUFF, Lt. S. D. 116th Bn., July 13th, 1918.
SCLATER, Lt. A. N., 13th Bn., July 18th, 1918.
IRVINE, Lieut. V. R., R.A.F. (missing), July 22nd, 1918.
GORDON, Lieut. J. A. R.F.A. (missing), July, 1918.
ALEXANDER, Gr. J. W., 54th Batty., August 7th, 1918.
HOYLES, Lt. (Maj.) H. L., 42nd Bn., August 8th, 1918.
THAIRS, Lt. E. F., 3rd Bn., Aug. 8th, 1918.
SCATCHERD, Lt. J. L., M.C., 11th Batt., Sept. 3rd, 1918.
CAMERON, Pte. Ken., 15th Bn., Sept., 1918.
WILSON, Lt. M. M., C.E.F., Oct. 10th, 1918.
HASTINGS, Lt. W. B., U.S.A., Oct. 16th, 1918.
CROSSLAND, Lt. E. F., R.A.F., Oct. 20, 1918.
DENNIS, Lt. H. O., 39th Bn., Oct., 1918.
COOPER, Pte Geo. O., Div. Cyclists, Oct., 1918.
HEIGHINGTON, Lt. Geof., 4th C.M.R., Nov. 2nd, 1918.
NICHOLSON, Lt. L. W., 4th C.M.R., Nov. 4th, 1918.
VAN STRAUBENZIE, Col. V. C., R.C.D., Nov., 1918.
RICHARDSON, Capt. Peter, at Coblenz, Feb. 15th, 1919.
WADSWORTH, Lieut. Livingstone, U.S.A.
FAIRFIELD, Gr. G. A., 1st C.F.A., May 19th, 1919.

Branches of the Old Boys' Association

DURING the year several branches of the Old Boys' Association have been formed, each with its own officers.
In January a meeting was held in Winnipeg, and the following account of it was clipped from one of the Winnipeg papers:

RIDLEY COLLEGE OLD BOYS ORGANIZE

A gathering of the Old Boys of Ridley College was held on
Saturday afternoon at the Manitoba Club, when it was decided
to organize a Western Branch of the Old Boys' Association, H. C.
Griffith, M.A., a member of the faculty, who is also an Old Boy,
came from St. Catharines to be present at the meeting. Mr. Griffith, in his address, referred to the Ridley Honor Roll, which con-
tained the names of 400 of the Old Boys serving at the front,
indicating the splendid showing made by the members of the
College.

Among those present at the meeting were Major Russell M.
McLeod, D. A. Wood, A. T. Wood, W. L. Billings, H. D. Gooderham,
Frank Bulling, L. R. Crawford, John Billings, Jr., Geo. B. Binns,
H. G. Wade, A. F. Douglas, F. Wright, G. D. Wood.

The election of officers resulted in H. Gerald Wade being
appointed president and H. D. Gooderham honorary secretary-
treasurer. Mr. Wade was appointed representative of the Western
Branch at the annual meeting of the Old Boys' organization in the
east.

MONTREAL

During the Easter holidays, Mr. Williams and Mr. Griffith
went to Montreal to attend the first dinner of the Montreal and
Quebec branch. The dinner was held at the St. James Club, and
was most successful. Among those present were Carl Riordon,
Colonel Rykert McCuaig, Major S. C. Norsworthy, Capt. C. N.
McCuaig, Lieut. J. Norsworthy, Capt. R. D. Gurd, Hal. Harmer, W.
Walbank, Harold Riordon, E. A. Wiggs (Quebec), M. D. Baldwin.
Letters of regret were read from several other Old Boys resident
in Montreal. The greatest enthusiasm for the School was ex-
pressed by all the speakers, and at the conclusion of the dinner,
a Montreal committee was chosen consisting of Carl Riordon,
Esq., chairman; Major S. C. Norsworthy, vice-chairman, and Capt.
Dr. R. D. Gurd, 556 Rockland avenue, Outremont, Secretary. It
was decided to make the dinner an annual event.

BUFFALO

In June a dinner was held in Buffalo and the Buffalo and
district branch was organized. At the dinner were Mr. Griffith,
G. G. Riselay, E. P. Pfohl (Niagara Falls), John Acheson, W. E.

Doherty, J. P. Hancock (Niagara Falls), H. Rosehill, E. M. Shore, W. J. Stone, L. P. McDougal, H. A. Bacon (Adams Basin), F. Newman, B. Hatch (Jamestown), Dr. J. McNett (Endicott, N.Y.) As at the other dinners, the greatest enthusiasm prevailed and at the close a committee was chosen consisting of E. G. Riselay, 739 Main Street, Buffalo, and E. P. Pfohl, Niagara Falls, N.Y. The Buffalo Branch decided to make the dinner an annual affair, and with such a good beginning they hope to have a most successful re-union next year.

The forming of these Branches is a splendid thing for the Old Boys' Association and in all probability several more will be formed before the end of the year.

THE MEMORIAL CHAPEL

It will be good news for Old Boys to learn that the committee felt enough encouraged by the response to this fund to instruct their architects, Sproatt and Rolf, of Toronto, to draw up plans for the building. The site decided upon is the northwest corner of the grounds and we can look forward with confidence to the beginning of active building operations in the course of a few months.

Only those who are actively engaged in raising this fund can appreciate the magnitude of the undertaking, and a very large sum of money is still required.

The committee desire to impress upon every Old Boy of Ridley the great necessity of his co-operation in raising the amount needed. If everyone does his share as nobly as those who have already subscribed, the total amount of $100,000 should soon be assured to the committeee. There is no limit, maximum or minimum, placed on the amount which may be subscribed by Old Boys, but when it is remembered that out of a total of 650 available Old Boys, some 425 enlisted, of whom sixty laid down their lives, some idea may be had of the tremendous work which your committee has undertaken for you.

OLD BOYS

We are able to add several other names to our Active Service List, Capt. Reilly (Niagara Falls), Lt. G. L. Burland (Montreal), Lt. Paul Johnson (U.S.A.), Cad. G. A. Forbes, R.A.F., Hespeler, Lieut. L. P. MacDougall (Buffalo), Lieut. John Dunn, U.S.A.

In no one term since the war have we been favored by so many Old Boy visitors, and on the occasion of the Old Boys' Cricket Match, several were present who had not been at their School for a number of years. Among those who came to see us

were: R. L. Peek, Sid Gartshore, Henry Gooderham, Reg. Jarvis,
"Jas." Abbott, Harold Drope, J. Boyd, Hugh McCulloch, Les.
McCulloch, Sherman Mix, Park Thompson, Jack Walton, C. Ash-
worth, P. Breithaupt, Alec. Forbes, Jack Goldie, Paul Addy, Jack
Smallman, Dr. Jimmy McNett, Ed. Riselay, Ray Fowler, Lloyd
Newman, E. Ehni, Laddie Cassels, Walter Caldicott, W. S. Green-
ing, R. M. Harcourt, Geo. Marks, A. W. Taylor, A. C. Kingstone,
Mr. Hern, Mr. Mel. Brock, Jack Salway, Tom Meritt, G. R. Marani,
"Mill" Jarvis, Colin Scatcherd, Don and Sam McAllister, Gordon
Mills, R. C. Lee, Ferdie Marani, Cadet Don MacDonald, Os. Glass,
Chas. Hyde, Gordon Phippen, Cadet Charlie Boultbee, K. Crom-
bie, G. Davis, Rev. Mr. Prince, Cadet Lewis, Fenton Sneed, Alec.
Porter, Gregory Merritt, Tom Rigby, Robt. O'Brian, A, L. Bishop,
L. F. Bishop, Norman Daniel, W. H. Heighington, Eric Lefroy,
J. M. Sutherland, Hollis Blake, H. H. Charles, G. G. Mitchell, Tom
Jenckes, John Lennox, A. F. Schram, H. W. Symmes, J. Turn-
bull, Norman Taylor, John Dunn, Dick Weaver, Allan Notman,
Hal. Williams.

SIGN POSTS ON THE HIGHWAY OF SCHOOL LIFE.

A dreary way to School.
Forty weeks to exams.
(Accessories—Brains, Vigor, Health and Youth).
Stop! Look! Listen!
Angry Master. Careful driving necessary.
Thirty minutes on the Latin road.
Difficult passage. Very narrow.
Detour to avoid detention.
Watch out for prefect.
End of term. Free air.
Last term. Very slippery. Look out.
Fifteen days to end. Up grade all the way.
Caution. Don't overheat engine.
Use plenty of oil. Keep to the right.
Holidays at last. Sucessful trip.
Not a puncture. General overhaul.

                                        —J. M. Bright, IIIA.

Master—Some of the gases in the air are argon, neon, kryp-
ton and so-on.

Mix and Hyslop in daily quarrel:
Mix.—Say, Hyslop, you're the biggest fool in this room!
Mr. K—p. (just entering)—Boys, you must not forget that I
am here.

LOWER SCHOOL SNAPS

PRIZE DAY

On Tuesday, June 24th, Ridley College completed the 30th year of her history, and the occasion was marked by a very suc-cessful "Prize Day."

Many out-of-town friends arrived in time for lunch, which was served in the dining-room, and afforded an excellent oppor-tunity for parents to become better acquainted with the Staff.

Afterwards in the Gymnasium, before a large audience, the various prize winners were called to the front to receive from the Bishop of Niagara the rewards of their successful efforts.

Dr. Miller, in his short address, spoke of the growth of the School, and the intimate co-ordination of School and home life, necessary for ideal results in education.

His Lordship the Bishop of Niagara, showed by his remarks the deep interest he has for the School, and all that it stands for, and we feel sure that Ridley has fewer more sincere friends.

Archdeacon Rennison was the last speaker, and although the day was very warm, his eloquent remarks were welcomed by all his hearers, who would willingly have had him continue at greater length.

Afternoon tea was afterwards served out-of-doors and brought to a close the most successful year in our history.

LOWER SCHOOL
Shell Form.

General Proficiency—Gerald Blake Memorial Scholarship and Gold Medal, Weatherston; Second Scholarship, Botterell; Extra Scholarship, Case.

English—Prize, Weatherston. Hon. mention, Case, Waters, Massie, Botterell, Lennox, Gray, Ingalls ma.

Mathematics—Prize, Weatherston. Hon. mention, Macdon-ald, Mather, Ingalls ma., Gates.

Latin and French—Prize, Weatherston. Hon. mention, Bot-terell, Case, Lennox, Arnott.

Writing—Prize, Wismer. Hon. Mention, Massie, Lennox, Waters.

Scripture and Divinity—Prize, Massie. Hon. mention, Mather, Arnott, Waters, Weatherston, Case.

UPPER SECOND FORM

General Proficiency—Prize, Brent.

English—Prize, Brent. Hon. mention, Millidge, Innes, Dafoe, Harrison.

Mathematics—Prize, Ridout. Hon. mention, Millidge, Harri-son, Innes, Brent.

Writing—Prize, Brent. Hon. mention, Dafoe, Innes.
Scripture and Divinity—Prize, Brent. Hon. mention, Millidge.

UPPER SECOND FORM
General Proficiency—1st, Wynn; 2nd, Biggar.
Scripture and Divinity—Prize, Biggar.

FIRST FORM
General Proficiency—1st, Stringer ma.; 2nd, Rogers.
Scripture and Divinity—Prize, Henderson. Hon. mention, Stringer ma.

SPECIAL PRIZES
Diligence, Arnott.
Punctuality—Arnott.
Neatness in Dormity—McCormack.
Batting Average—Macdonald.
Bowling Average—Lennox.
Fielding—McCormack.

UPPER SCHOOL
SPECIAL PRIZES
Principal's Reading Prize—Osborne.
Speaking—I., Prize by Col Merritt—Norsworthy.
Speaking—II., Prize by A. C. Kingstone—Stringer ma. Special Junior, Greentree.
Manliness—Glass.
Essay (Mrs. Leonard's Prize)—Weaver.
Batting Average—Barr, 31.5—Special Bat (for 55 not out in School game). Prize by Mr. H. N. Baird.
Bowling—Somerville I., 6.7.
Fielding—MacHahon. Prize by Dr. Adam Wright.
Shooting—Bertram, O'Brian.
Diligence—Snyder.

FORM V.
General Proficiency—Biggar I. Prize by J. H. Ingersoll.
English—Biggar I., Coleman mi., Snyder.
Fernch and German—Biggar I.
Latin and Greek—Cronyn, Williams.
History—Cronyn, Shearson.
Mathematics—Biggar I.
Science—Coleman mi., Harrison mi.
Scripture—Wainwright, Biggar I.

FORM IVA.
English—Pearson, Biggar II.
Mathematics and Science—Biggar II., Osler ma.
Latin and Greek—Biggar II., Osler ma.
French—Biggar II., Osler ma.

History and Geography—Glassco, Orme.
Reading—Douglas.
Scripture—Glassco, Biggar II.
General Proficiency (Gerald Blake Memorial Scholarship)—
Biggar II., Osler ma.

FORM IVB.
English—Hansard, Carter.
Mathematics and Science—Pierce, Smith and Leigh.
Latin and Greek—Hansard, Pierce.
French—Hansard.
History and Geography—Pierce.
Reading—Carter and Butler.
Scripture—Butler.
General Proficiency (Gerald Blake Memorial Scholarship)—
Hansard, Pierce.

FORM IIIA.
Lit., Gram. and Comp.—Pope, Osler mi.
Maths. and Science—Osler mi., Budder and Price.
Latin and French—Budden.
History and Geography—Greentree, Bright mi.
Reading—Fairbanks, Kerr.
Writing—Gledhill, Bryan ma.
Scripture—Bright mi., Budden.
General Proficiency—Budden.

FORM IIIB.
Latin, Grammar and Composition—Sims, Turnbull.
Mathematics and Science—Turnbull, Breckenridge.
Latin and French—Turnbull, Breckenridge.
History and Geography—Tebbs, Turnbull.
Reading—Sims, Perkins.
Writing—Shurley, Le Page.
Scripture—Perkins, Tebbs.
General Proficiency—Turnbull.

———

Mr. P——.—What is a fixed star?
Pupil—One that stays stalled.

———

I wonder if a minister could marry himself?
No, he must marry a woman.

———

Pupil—I can't learn languages.
Master—You can learn the "Butting-in" language very well.
Pupil—Who teaches that, sir?

———

I was here in spirit before the days of prohibition.

The Cadet Corps

The work of the Corps throughout the early part of the year was not quite so good as usual, but during the past term no such criticism could be offered. Every Cadet did his best, and by inspection day, the Corps was in first-class condition.

The Inspecting Officer was Col. Barker, who was assisted by Col. McCordick of St. Catharines. Promptly at three o'clock, the Corps formed in line for the general salute, after which uniforms and equipment were carefully inspected, and found to be, without exception, in excellent condition.

The "March Past" followed, and was never better done by any Ridley Corps, calling forth from the spectators hearty applause.

Company Drill, by Glass the Company leader, showed the work of the Corps as a whole, and was well done.

Platoon Drill, by Platoon Commanders Hamilton I. and Soanes followed, and again the work of officers and cadets came in for well-deserved praise.

Section Drill, under Section Commanders Weaver, Coleman ma., MacMahon and Stringer, was particularly interesting, and Mr. A. W. Taylor's prize for the best all-round section went to No. I. under Weaver, with No. III., under MacMahon, only a fraction of a point behind. Sections II. and IV. were tie, just one point behind No. III.

Physical Drill, under Company Leader Glass was about the most interesting event on the programme, and the many movements were executed smartly and in excellent time.

The attack brought the inspection to a close, and under a wonderful smoke screen the attacking force succeeded in reaching a point of vantage without serious loss, notwithstanding heavy artillery and machine gun fire.

The final charge was a great success, and all objectives were gained on schedule time.

The work of the Band, under Barr, and Signal Corps, under Reid II., came in for much praise, and Col. Barker, in his address to the Corps, included them specifically when stating that he had never inspected a better balanced corps.

Altogether we have every reason to be proud of this year's corps, and their work so pleased the Inspecting Officer that he suggested that a representation be sent to the Canadian National Exhibition during the latter part of August.

Before adjourning for refreshments, Glass called for cheers for the King, Col. Barker and Col. Thairs, and the response to the last, we are free to confess, might have made the King himself envious, so hearty and spontaneous was it.

CORPS AT THE EXHIBITION

Following out the suggestion made by Col. Barker, that the Ridley College Cadet Corps be represented at the C.N.E. in Toronto this summer, it has been decided to send a section. Those selected will, we know, do their utmost to keep up our fine reputation, and we are expecting great things from them. The following boys will represent Ridley: Somerville I., Cronyn, Coleman mi., Snyder, Wainwright, Goldie, Johnson II., Orme, Tebbs, Kingston, Shurley, McLaren, Pearson, Greening ma., with Soanes and Glass in charge.

CADET INSPECTION REPORT.

The following is the official report sent to Col. Thairs by the Inspecting Officer, Col. R. K. Barker. It speaks for itself, and we are more than pleased that the Corps has again succeeded in doing so well:—

Personnel

1. Officers. State of efficiency. Very good. Do they command and assist in the instruction of their companies? Yes, very well.
2. Rank and file—general appearance and physique. Very smart, good physique.
3. Instructor, name, rank and Corps, Lieut.-Col. Thairs, R.O. His qualifications. F. O. Cert.
4. Explanation as to absentees. Two sick.

Material

5. Where are arms kept? Remarks—in rink annex, cupboard and racks.
6. Arms and stores, condition. Very good.
7. Describe uniform worn and state condition. Rifles, green tunics, breeches, puttees and forage caps.
8. Books. Are the latest editions of the necessary books in possession of the Instructor, Cadet Officers and Company? Yes.

Training Performed

9. Physical Training. Very good, all Cadets daily.
10. Scout training—Signalling, very good.
11. Infantry Training Section drill, excellent. Platoon drill, very good. Company drill, excellent. Skirmishing, very good. Company field training, very good. Attack with smoke screen defence Ceremonial (if any), very good. Musketry exercises, very good.
12. Musketry and judging distance. Remarks on scores made, returns inspected, and instructions given during the year. All Cadets firing. Several 30 out of possible 35.
13. General remarks. Best trained, smartest and cleanest Cadet Corps I have yet inspected.
14. Is any special assistance rendered by School Board or other local body? Yes, uniforms, cupboards, bugle band instruments.

THE DANCING CLASS

During the past term we were privileged to have a dancing class in our midst. The class was held in the Dean's House library on Friday evening through the kindness of Mr. Powell. Miss

Rigby, our teacher, brought up from 10 to 15 girls each Friday evening, whose presence was much appreciated. The boys made remarkable progress in the time at their disposal, due to the splendid teaching of Miss Rigby and the help of the girls. The class was brought to a very successful close when on the last night the boys entertained the girls. Refreshments were served and formed a fitting climax to the most successful evening of the term. The following boys were in the class: Counsell ma., Cook, Steacy, McTaggart, Gledhill, Fairbank, Sims, Turnbull, Eliot, Carter, Warren, Macy, Mosher, Bryan mi.　　　　Carter IV.B.

THE STORE

Not far away from here,
　　On a corner of a street,
There is a little store,
　　That is very trim and neat.

And to this little place,
　　We are often seen to speed;
When we have a little money
　　And need a little feed.

They sell us rosy apples,
　　Ice cream and ginger beer.
And often when we leave the place
　　We feel and look quite queer.

But this little place we love,
　　And we couldn't do without,
For how can any Ridley boy
　　Subsist on college trout?
　　　　　　　—Kertland, IVA.

"WHAT CAN YOU DO?"

Weep and you're called a baby,
　　Laugh, and you'rs called a fool.
Yield and you're called a coward,
　　Stand and you're called a mule.
Smile, and they'll call you silly,
　　Frown, and they call you gruff.
Put on a front like a millionaire
　　And somebody calls your bluff.　　　　—Exchange

THE SUPPER

The voting in class, after study, turned out,
At the cross-country supper, that I'd have to spout.
So I worked up some notes, —I had only one day,
And t'was certainly hard to find something to say.

So the supper was finished, they all seemed so gay
But my knees were quite shakey (they had been all day)
I stood up and spoke, it wasn't so bad,
But when it was finished, I surely was glad.
　　　　　　　C. A. H. IV.

RIDLEY COLLEGE CRICKET ELEVEN, 1919
Inter-School Champions.

OFFICERS OF THE CADET CORPS

INSPECTION

Every morn and every night
   The Corps turned out to drill.
The Colonel tried with all his might
   The fine points to instill.

He made us do each move just right
   Before we were dismissed.
For honours high were just in sight,
   Our Corps must head the list.

Our belts must all be polished bright—
   Our uniforms without a spot,
Our rifles clean from butt to sight,
   Of work, it took a lot.

In Swedish Drill, we hoped for praise,
   And practiced hard each day.
The Bugle Band its calls did raise
   To Heaven, the neighbors say.

The Signallers not to be outdone,
   Sent messages afar.
And on inspection day they shone
   Their work well over par.

And so we worked from morn till night,
   That when inspection came,
We might once more obtain the right
   To claim our usual fame.

          —Turnbull IIIB.

Waiting for the next victim   Umpiring in the rain

Mr. C——.—What is the capital of Turkey?

E——lma.——Showing some hesitation.

Mr. C——.—What part of the question is troubling you?

E——lma.—No part, sir. It's the answer.

TERM DIARY

April 23—Everybody back, almost.
    25—Disturbance at Vth. form table.—Reid.
    28—Cricket starts.
    29—R. L. Peek back.
May 8—Sid Gartshore visits us.
    10—School sees the "Better 'Ole." Le Page, Mosher and
        McLennan don't.
    11—Reid does some house-cleaning on flat—rugs princi-
        pally.
    12—H. Gooderham here.
    17—Ridley 105, Albions 56. First game.
    18—Capt. Macdonald in Chapel. "Reg" Jarvis back.
    20—Eliot mi. leaves for France.
    21—"Jas." Abbott and Harold Drope here.
    23—J. Boyd, McCulloch Bros., Mix., Thomson, Walton and
        Ashworth here. Forster in an undress parade.
    24—O. C. O. 47, Ridley 44.
    26—John Goldie and Babe McCulloch here.
    27—Woodruff wins "mile."
    28—Paul Addy here.
    30—Sports day. Champions, Woodruff (Sr.), MacWhinney
        (Inter.), Shurly (Jr.).
    31—Yorkshire 100, Ridley 48. "The Masters and the Maids."
June 1—Church parade. Great success.
    2—Tim's dog goes to the Happy Hunting Ground.
    3—No holiday. How disloyal!
    6—Alf. plays Sir Galahad; R.M.C. "graduates" leave.
    7—Old Boys' game—close game, 135 tie.
    8—Rev. Moore, formerly Chaplain 3rd Brigade, in Chapel.
    9—Circus, some attraction (Sparks).
    11—Ridley wins four games of cricket.
    14—Ridley 105 for 5; St. Andrew's 46. Barr gets a "lamp."
    15—Haverford, arrives.
    16—Ridley defeats Haverford.
    21—Ridley defeats U. C. C.
    23—Ridley defeats T. C. S. Champions again.
    24—Prize day. School closes.
    25—Masters still working.
July 12—Acta out.
    18—Matric. exams over. Hurrah!

Lightning Source UK Ltd.
Milton Keynes UK
UKHW012015021218
333216UK00014B/2471/P